How To Delegate
Work and Responsibility

A Step by Step Guide to
Effective Delegation Techniques

I0462913

By Meir Liraz

Published by BizMove
www.bizmove.com

Table of Contents

1. Introduction

Delegating work, responsibility, and authority is difficult in a company because it means letting others make decisions which involve spending the owner-manager's money. At a minimum, you should delegate enough authority to get the work done, to allow assistants to take initiative, and to keep the operation moving in your absence.

This Guide discusses controlling those who carry responsibility and authority and coaching them in self-improvement. It emphasizes the importance of allowing competent assistants to perform in their own style rather than insisting that things be done exactly as the owner-manager would personally do them.

"Let others take care of the details."

That, in a few words, is the meaning of delegating work and responsibility.

In theory, the same principles for getting work done through other people apply whether you have 25 employees and one top assistant or 150 to 200 employees and several managers. Yet, putting the principles into practice is often difficult.

Delegation is perhaps the hardest job owner-managers have to learn. Some never do. They insist on handling many details and work themselves into early graves. Others pay lip service to the idea but actually run a one-man shop. They give their assistants many responsibilities but little or no authority.

2. How Much Authority?

Authority is the fuel that makes the machine go when you delegate work and responsibility. It poses a question: To what extent do you allow another person to make decisions which involve spending your company's money?

That question is not easy to answer. Sometimes, an owner-manager has to work it out as he goes along, as did Tom Brasser. His pride in being the top man made it hard for him to share authority. He tried, but he found to his dismay that his delegating was not as good as he thought.

One day when he returned from his first short business trip. Mr. Brasser stormed out of his office. He waved a sheaf of payroll sheets and shouted "Who approved all this overtime while I was away?" I did," the production chief answered.

Realizing that all heads were turned to see what the shouting was about., Mr. Brasser lowered his voice. Taking the production manager with him, he stepped into his office.

There he told the production man, "You've got your nerve authorizing overtime. This is still my company, and I'll decide what extra costs we'll take on. You know good and well that our prices are not based on paying overtime rates."

"Right," the production man replied. "But you told me I was in full charge of production. You said I should keep pushing so I wouldn't fall behind on deliveries."

"That's right," Mr. Brasser said. "In fact, I recall writing you about a couple of orders just before I went out of town."

"You can say that again. And one of them - the big order - was getting behind so I approved overtime."

"I would have done the same thing if I has been here," Mr. Brasser said. "But let's get things straight for the future. From now on, overtime needs my okay. We've got to keep costs in line."

Mr. Brasser then followed up with his other department heads, including his office manager and purchasing agent. He called them in, told them what had happened, and made it clear that their authority did not include making decisions that would increase the company's operating costs. Such decisions had to have his approval, he pointed out, because it was his company. He was the one who would lose, if and when, increased costs ate up the profit.

Yet, if an owner-manager is to run a successful company, you must delegate authority properly. How much authority is proper depends on your situation.

At a minimum, you should delegate enough authority:

(1) To get the work done,

(2) To allow key employees to take initiative, and

(3) To keep things going in your absence.

3. To Whom Do You Delegate?

Delegation of responsibility does not mean that you say to your assistants, "Here, you run the shop." The people to whom you delegate responsibility and authority must be competent in the technical areas for which you hold them accountable. However, technical competence is not enough.

In addition, the person who fills a key management spot in the organization must either be a manager or be capable of becoming one. A manager's chief job is to plan, direct, and coordinate the work of others.

A manager should possess the three "I's" - initiative, interest, and imagination. The manager of a department must have enough self-drive to start and keep things moving. A manager should not have to be told, for example, to make sure that employees start work on time.

Personality traits must be considered. A key manager should be strong- willed enough to overcome opposition when necessary and should also have enough ego to want to "look good" but not so much that it antagonizes other employees.

4. Spell Out the Delegation

Competent people want to know for what they are being held responsible. The experience of Charles P. Wiley illustrates how one owner-manager let them know. He started by setting up an organization. He broke his small company into three departments: a production department, a sales department, and an administrative department.

The manager who handled production was responsible for advertising, customer solicitations, and customer service. Mr. Wiley regarded the administrative department as the headquarters and service unit for the other two. Its manager was responsible for personnel, purchasing, and accounting.

Mr. Wiley also worked out with his assistants the practices and procedures necessary to get the jobs done. His assistants were especially helpful in pointing out any overlaps or gaps in assigned responsibilities. He then put the procedures into writing. Thus each supervisor had a detailed statement of the function of each's department and the extent of each's authority.

This statement included a list of specific actions

which they could take on their own initiative and a list of actions which required approval in the front office - Mr. Wiley, or in his absence, the assistant general manager.

Mr. Wiley had thought about the times when he might be absent from the plant. To make sure that things would keep moving, the production manager was designated assistant general manager and given authority to make all operational decisions in Mr. Wiley's absence.

In thinking about absences, Mr. Wiley went one step further. He instructed each department head to designate and train an assistant who could run the department if, and when, the need arose.

When you spell out the delegation, be sure that departments are coordinated. The experience of another small plant owner, Ann Jones, is a case in point. She thought her departments were coordinated until the shop manager reported that he was swamped with "rush" orders.

"It's impossible for me to make good on Bill's promise," the shop chief said. Bill was the sales manager.

When Bill was called in, he said "I had to promise early delivery to get the business."

Ms. Jones resolved the problem by instructing the sales manager and the shop manager to work out delivery dates together.

Make sure that departments are coordinated when you spell out the responsibilities and authority of each key manager. Thus you reduce the chances of confusion as well as assuring that there is no doubt about who is responsible for specific jobs. Then, the particular key manager can take corrective action before things get out of hand.

5. Keeping Control

When you manage through others, it is essential that you keep control. You do it by holding a subordinate responsible for his or her actions and checking the results of those actions.

In controlling your assistants, try to strike a balance. You should not get into a key manager's operation so closely that you stifle him or her should you be so far removed that you lose control of things.

You need feedback to keep yourself informed. Reports provide a way to get the right kind of feedback at the right time. They can be daily, weekly, or monthly, depending on how soon you need the information. Each department head can report his or her progress, or the lack of it, in the unit of production that is appropriate for his or her activity; for example, items packed in the shipping room, sales per territory, hours of work per employee.

Periodic staff meetings are another way to get feedback. At these meetings, department heads can comment on their activities, accomplishments, and problems.

6. Coaching Your Staff

For the owner-manager, delegation does not end with good control. It involves coaching as well, because management ability is not acquired automatically. You have to teach it.

Just as important, you have to keep your managers informed just as you would be if you were doing their jobs. Part of your job is to see that they get the facts they need for making their decisions.

You should be certain that you convey your thinking when you coach your assistants. Sometimes words can be inconsistent with your thoughts. Ask questions to make sure the listener understands your meanings. In other words, delegation can only be effective when you have good communications.

And above all, listen. Many owner-managers get so involved in what they are saying or are going to say next, that they do not listen to the other person. In coaching a person so he or she can improve, it is important to tell why you give the instruction.

When a person knows the reason, he or she is better able to supervise.

7. Allow Staff to Work

Sometimes you find yourself involved in many operational details even though you do everything that is necessary for delegating responsibility. In spite of defining authority, delegating to competent persons, spelling out the delegation, keeping control, and coaching, you are still burdened with detailed work. Why? Usually, you have failed to do one vital things. You have refused to stand back and let the wheels turn.

If you are to make delegation work, you must allow your managers freedom to do things their way. You and the company are in trouble if you try to measure your assistants by whether or not they do a particular task exactly as you would do it. They should be judged by their results - not their methods.

No two persons react exactly the same in every situation. Be prepared to see some action taken differently from the way in which you would do it even though your policies are well defined. Of course, if an assistant strays too far from policy, you need to bring him or her back into line. You cannot afford second-guessing.

You should also keep in mind that when an owner-manager second-guesses assistants, you risk destroying their self-confidence. If the assistant does not run his or her department to your satisfaction and if his or her department to your satisfaction and if his or her shortcomings cannot be overcome, then replace that person. But when results prove his or her effectiveness, it is good practice to avoid picking at each move he or she makes.

8. Effective Supervisory Practices

If an employee's job satisfies his or her needs, the employee responds more favorably to the job. This may happen, for example, when an employee is given the responsibility for managing the office on his or her own, and is recognized for doing it well. Or it may occur when a sales representative is assigned full responsibility for developing new business as well as maintaining existing customers in a territory and is recognized for the accomplishment. Such employees tend to take their responsibilities seriously, act positively for the firm, and are absent from work only rarely.

The key point is that when a job satisfies needs, the employee may bring greater commitment to the job. Some needs common to all individuals are basics like food, shelter, and security for the future. Normally a fair wage level and a feeling of security that the job will continue, tend to satisfy these needs. Such needs, however, can be satisfied in most jobs today, and they do not alone evoke heavy commitment by employees to your firm.

Other needs must also be satisfied. Most of these are related to:

a. The firm's personnel practices such as complaint handling or vacation scheduling

b. Working conditions

c. Supervisory practices such as discipline, or the way instructions are given, and

d. Total compensation, including benefits practices.

If what the firm provides in any of these aspects is seen by the employees as much poorer than what other firms in the area provide, dissatisfactions will result. On the other hand, improvements above an acceptable level generally do not bring about greater employee commitment in the long run.

For example, total disregard for employee complaints (personnel practices) can lead to serious problems for the firm. When employee complaints are handled well, serious problems tend to be precluded from developing but there is no major gain in deep employee commitment to the job.

What then does bring about a serious commitment to the job and firm?

There are five factors that generally cause a deep commitment to job performance for most employees. These are:

1. The work itself - to what extent does the employee see the work as meaningful and worthwhile?

2. Achievement - how much opportunity is there for the employee to accomplish tasks that are seen as a reasonable challenge?

3. Responsibility - to what extent does the employee have assignment and the authority necessary to take care of a significant function of the organization?

4. Recognition - to what extent is the employee aware of how highly other people value the contributions made by the employee?

5. Advancement - how much opportunity is there for the employee to assume greater responsibilities in the firm?

These five factors tend to satisfy certain critical needs of individuals:

One need is the feeling of being accepted as part of the firm's work-team.

Another need is for feeling important - that the

employee's strengths, capabilities and contributions are known and valued highly.

A third need is for the chance to continue to grow and become a more fully functioning person.

If the kinds of needs just described are met by paying attention to the five factors previously listed, an owner/manager will have taken significant steps toward gaining the full commitment of employees to job performance. To do this, several practical strategies can be used, such as:

Establishing confidence and trust with your employees through open communication and the development of sensitivity to employee needs

Allowing employees participation in decision-making which directly affects them

Helping employees to set their own work methods and work goals, as much as possible

Praising and rewarding good work as clearly and promptly as inadequate performance is mentioned

Restructuring jobs to be challenging and interesting by giving increased responsibilities and independence to those who want it, and who can handle it